LADAKH

THE LIFE JOURNEY

ABHISHEK LONKAR

Contents

Acknowledgements

Writing this book has been a journey as enriching as the travels it recounts. I am deeply grateful to all those who supported and inspired me throughout this endeavor.

First and foremost, I would like to thank my younger brother, Nikhil, whose technical support was invaluable in bringing this project to life. From solving tech glitches to guiding me through formatting and digital aspects, his help made the process much smoother. My family and relatives for their constant encouragement and belief in my vision.

To my friends and fellow travelers, Gaurav, Suraj, Nilesh, Sumedh who shared stories, laughter, and memories on the road – thank you for being part of the adventure. Your presence is woven into every page.

Lastly, to the readers- thank you for embarking on this journey with me. I hope this book inspires you to chase your own adventures and find joy in the unexpected.

CHAPTER ONE

AIM: KEEP IT ALIVE

I have travelled around the world- from the vibrant cities of India to the elegance of Paris, the serene beauty of Switzerland, the buzz of Tokyo, the glamour of Dubai, the charm of Mauritius, and the cultural richness of places like Kodaikanal, Gir forest, Tamil Nadu, Kerala, Madhya Pradesh , Goa, Maharashtra, Rajasthan but Ladakh was something else entirely, it was different. It touched my soul in a way no other pace had.

Even after the trip ended, something still felt missing. I had a lingering void inside me – a feeling I needed to put into words the old-school way. Writing this book became the perfect outlet for that emotion. Each page I wrote felt like revisiting a memory, a moment that deserved to live beyond the silence of my thoughts. The laughter, the roads, the silence of the mountains – all of it kept echoing in my heart. I wasn't just documenting a journey; I was healing through it, trying to make sense of why it touched me so deeply.

"Sometime, the journey doesn't end when the road does. Sometimes, it continues within you- and this book is that continuation."

In the quiet moments after the trip, I often found myself drifting back – to the crisp mountain air, the shared glances between friends when words fell short, the thrill of uncertain paths, and the peace that only a place like Ladakh could offer.

It wasn't just about the landscapes or the winding roads through the Himalayas. It wasn't even about the adventure or the photos we clicked along the way. It was something subtler, a quiet awakening. The kind that doesn't shout but lingers like the thin mountains air that refuses to fill your lungs the first few days. Maybe it was the conversation we had under the star, or the long silences that said more than words ever could. Maybe it was realizing how small we really are when we're surrounded by something so vas, so untouched, so brutally honest.

CHAPTER TWO

THE SPARK

What started as a casual conversation among late-20s friends turned into the adventure of a lifetime memory.

It was a regular evening—five friends, a familiar hangout spot, and the comfort of old jokes and endless laughter. The sun had dipped below the horizon, and as usual, we were just sitting around, enjoying each other's company after a long day. That's when Gaurav casually threw out the idea that would change everything:

"Guys, we should do a bike trip to Ladakh."

At first, it sounded like one of those impulsive, half-serious plans that people talk about but never follow through. But that night was different. The moment Gaurav said it, something clicked. One by one, heads turned. No one laughed it off or changed the topic. Instead, there was a pause—a kind of silent agreement—and then I nodded, followed by Suraj, Nilesh, and Sumedh.

What started as a random suggestion quickly turned serious. Within three weeks, the idea picked up momentum. We were all in. The original plan was to go in May, but we had to postpone it to **17th July 2024**, since Sumedh had to appear for his PG (medical) exams in June.

It worked out, though. According to Google, July is actually one of the best months to visit Ladakh.

Now that we had extra time, we dove into planning and preparation. Every month, we met to discuss latest ideas and update our itinerary. Our excitement only grew.

The initial idea was simple: take a direct flight from Pune to Leh. But we soon realized there were no direct flights. The next best option was from Mumbai. We found a direct flight from Mumbai to Leh—about a three-hour journey. Being a group of five, we noticed the flight prices increasing day by day, so we quickly booked our tickets with **IndiGo Airlines** at ₹10,745 per person.

With travel confirmed, we shifted our focus to **gear and essentials**. High-altitude travel demands respect—especially if you're riding bikes through mountain passes like **Khardung La** and **Chang La**. We needed proper gear: **riding jackets, thermal layers, gloves, helmets, hydration packs, and sturdy shoes**.

Everyone was busy buying their gear. I didn't need to get much—I had already bought most of my things in advance. So naturally, I became the unofficial guide, helping the others with their purchases and giving tips from my own past experiences.

And just like that, the dream started taking shape.

Everything was going perfectly—until it wasn't.

On the night of **22nd June**, just a few weeks before our trip, I got an unexpected call from Nilesh around **10:00 PM**. He sounded serious and asked me to meet him in Kharadi, where he was already with Sumedh. I didn't ask many questions—I just got on my bike and went.

As soon as I reached, I could sense something was off. The first words I heard were:
"The exam has been postponed."

My mind froze for a second. The **PG exam** that Sumedh was supposed to give the next day—**23rd June**—had been cancelled due to a paper leak. Just like that, all the dates and planning we'd done were hanging in midair. Sumedh didn't know the new exam date yet, but he was clear about one thing:
"I'm still in for the trip."

He was frustrated and helpless, and honestly, so were we. It wasn't fair—not to him, not to us. But this was something completely out of our control. We had no backup plan. Nothing. That night, we just decided to wait for a week and hope that the new exam date would be announced soon.

Meanwhile, I threw myself into preparation. At the peak of my excitement, I worked on a **detailed 12-day itinerary** for both Ladakh and Himachal. I calculated travel times, sorted routes, and highlighted all the must-visit spots—monasteries, lakes, mountain passes. Everything. I even divided time for rest, food stops, and scenic viewpoints. It felt like the perfect plan for an epic ride.

The next weekend, we planned to meet again—this time in **Magarpatta**—to take a final call. But that day, **Nilesh didn't show up.** When we called, he said he wasn't feeling well. At first, it seemed like just a viral fever. Nothing too serious. He said he'd recover in two days. So, we kept the discussion going without him.

And then, **another blow.**

Sumedh finally said the words we didn't want to hear:
"I don't think I can continue."

There was silence for a moment. He wasn't quitting because he wanted to. He was genuinely uncertain. The exam could happen anytime, and this was his future. None of us wanted to pressure him. We respected his decision.

Now, one rider down, the plan needed serious rethinking. I spoke to Gaurav and said,
"Maybe we should skip Himachal altogether."

The weather reports from Himachal were terrible—**cloudbursts, landslides, road closures.** Riding 1,500+ kilometres through that was risky. Gaurav agreed. It was starting to feel like the mountains were evaluating our will.

Just when we thought things were settling again, I received another call from Nilesh—this time with some unwelcome news.

It wasn't viral fever. It was dengue.

I couldn't believe what I was hearing. There was **just one week left** for our departure, and now another rider was down. I went numb for a moment, then just told him to rest, not to worry, and take care of himself. But inside, I was shaken. This trip, our dream, was starting to collapse one piece at a time.

That evening, **Gaurav, Suraj, and I met again**, just the three of us. Gaurav looked at me and asked, **"What should we do now?"**

I looked him straight in the eye and said, **"I don't care if it's just me—I'm going. Alone if I have to."**

That one sentence changed everything.

Gaurav's face lit up. That confidence gave him a push, and Suraj followed. In that moment, it became clear—the trip was still alive. Not with five, not even four. But **three of us** were still standing.

That night, we sat down and drafted a brand new **15-day itinerary**, cutting Himachal completely and focusing entirely on Ladakh. The route changed, the mood changed, but the spirit remained the same.

The journey was back on. Smaller in number, but stronger in resolve.

With just days to go, and the group now down to three, we weren't discouraged—we were focused. If anything, we were more determined to make every day of this journey count. The plan had changed, but Ladakh was still calling.

We sat down once again to draw up a **new itinerary**, this time focusing fully on the **Ladakh circuit**. It would still be the adventure of a lifetime—just with fewer people, and sharper intentions.

Our updated route looked like this:

- **2 days acclimatizing in Leh.**
- **2 days in Hunder Village (Nubra Valley)**
- **2 days at Pangong Lake**
- **2 days in Hanle (near the Indo-China border)**
- **2 days in Zanskar Valley**
- **2 days to explore Leh city**
- Then fly out from **Leh to Delhi on 29**[th] **July.**
- Spend **2 days in Delhi!**
- Finally, return to **Pune.**

We were lucky that we hadn't pre-booked round-trip flights. We had only booked **one-way flights** so far, which gave us the flexibility to adjust our return based on the new plan. On **15**[th] **July**, just two days before departure, we met and finalized all hotel bookings.

Here's where we chose to stay:

- **Leh** – *Ladakh Himalayan Retreat*
- **Nubra Valley** – *Himalayan Bunker*
- **Pangong Lake** – *Rangjon Resort*
- **Hanle** – *Padma Homestay*

With hotels booked and the revised route locked in; we also confirmed our return:

- **Flight from Leh to Delhi** on **29**[th] **July**
- **Flight from Delhi to Pune** after spending a couple of days exploring the capital.

- On **17**[th] **July**, at **6:30 PM**, we were standing at **Pune Railway Station**, bags on our backs, buzzing with energy. The three of us—**Suraj, Gaurav, and I**—were finally on our way.

Suraj and I were packed light—each of us had **one trekking backpack**. But **Gaurav... he came prepared like he was shifting homes.** He had **four bags**: a trekking backpack, a helmet bag, a jacket bag, and a handbag. We couldn't help but laugh, but we also felt for him—**he'd be carrying all that through crowded train stations and airports.**

Our **train to Mumbai** was an **intercity express**, and by **9:30 PM**, we reached **Dadar Station**. From there, we navigated the **Mumbai local trains**, switching lines to reach **Santa Cruz** station. The energy in Mumbai, even late at night, was electrifying.

Suraj and Gaurav had dinner. I was fasting that day, so I grabbed a quick **milkshake** to keep me going. By midnight, we were heading toward the **Mumbai Airport Terminal**.

After checking in our luggage and clearing security, we had a long layover—**around 8 to 9 hours** at the airport. But honestly, airports are never boring when you're excited. We found some comfortable seats, sat facing the runway, and just watched the magic happen—**planes taking off and landing**, lights flickering on the wet tarmac, and rain tapping gently against the windows.

It was **monsoon season**, and by **3:00 AM**, the skies opened up. Heavy rain lashed the runway, but inside, we felt calm, content, and incredibly alive.

We were finally here—**on the edge of our biggest adventure yet**.

At **7:30 AM**, our flight took off.

**"It only takes one spark
To light a fire inside you"**

CHAPTER THREE

TOUCHING THE SKY – ARRIVAL IN LEH

Our flight to Leh was scheduled for **7:30 AM**, and the **Mumbai monsoon was in full swing** that morning. As we sat inside the plane, watching the heavy rain batter the runway, I honestly thought we'd be delayed. The sky was covered in thick clouds, visibility was poor, and the mood was tense.

But once we were in the air, everything changed.

About two hours into the flight, as we began crossing into Kashmir, the **clouds opened up**, and what we saw next took our breath away. Below us were the mighty **Himalayas**, blanketed in snow and glowing in the morning sun. Glaciers cut across the ridges like silver veins, and for the first time, we saw the raw scale of the **mountain kingdom we were entering**.

As we approached Leh, the **view of the city from above** was stunning—**monasteries, palaces, clinging to cliffs**, barren mountains rising like waves, and the tight grid of Leh town nestled quietly below. At **10:30 AM**, we touched down at **Kushok Bakula Rimpochee Airport**.

The air was sharp and cool. Not freezing, but fresh in a way that city air never is. The airport itself was small—**almost dreamlike**, surrounded by mountains on all sides, like a secret base carved out just for adventurers.

We were picked up and dropped at our hotel, the **Ladakh Himalayan Retreat**, and honestly—it turned out to be one of the best hotels. Comfortable, quiet, and with views of the hills that instantly made us feel at peace.

For me travelling to Leh felt Like stepping into dreamscape carved by nature and time. As you travel through winding mountain roads every turn offers breathtaking taking view-barren yet beautiful landscapes, towering peaks, and valleys. Reaching leh you're greeted by crispy mountain air and the charm of a town that feels timeless. The narrow streets bustle with local life, and the aroma of Tibetan food drifts from small cafes.

Since we had flown in, **acclimatization was absolutely necessary**. Everyone is advised to take at least 24–48 hours to let their bodies adjust to the **11,500 ft altitude**, and we followed that strictly.

Later that day, we contacted **Padma Bhai from Toro Ladakh Adventure**, our trusted local bike rental partner. And that's when I met the beast—**the Royal Enfield Himalayan 411**.

I had never ridden this bike before. It stood tall, rugged, and ready for war. And once I got on it, everything changed. The Himalayan 411 wasn't just a motorcycle—it was a partner. **Stable, solid, and made for mountains**, it felt like it belonged to this land. I was instantly hooked. I had new respect for the machine, and I knew—this trip was going to be different.

That evening, we took a short walk to a nearby café to taste the local Flavors. We ordered **momos** and **thukpa**, a warm noodle soup that hit the spot. Sitting in that café, sipping hot soup as the chilly wind blew through the valley, it finally hit us: **We were in Ladakh. The dream was real.**

As night fell, Leh revealed its second form—**pure silence**. No honking, no engines, just the occasional bark of a dog or flutter of prayer flags. The stars came out in thousands. That night, we stayed up till **1:30 AM**, just talking. About the ride. About life. About how far we'd come.

The next morning, we got up early and went out for breakfast in Leh's **Old City**. All three of us ordered an **English breakfast**, but what arrived was closer to a full meal—massive portions, warm toast, eggs, sausages, beans, and local butter. Exactly what we needed.

Our first destination that day was the **Magnetic Hill**, about **30 kilometres** from Leh. The roads were smooth, winding, and fun to ride, but honestly—**the spot itself felt overhyped**. It was packed with tourists, and we didn't really experience any magnetic force. Just a marked stretch of road, and a lot of expectations.

While returning from magnetic hill, we made a memorable stop at the hall of fame in Leh. This museum, dedicated to the brave soldiers who had lost their lives through the Indo-pak wars, OP Vijay of Kargil war, the soldiers who lost their lives in Siachen glacier. Offered a moving glimpse into the sacrifices made in service to the nation. Then went to café for some refreshment.

By afternoon, we returned to the hotel for rest.

One thing we noticed immediately—**Leh gets a surprising amount of sunlight** during summer. Even at **6:00 PM**, it felt like it was just 4:00 PM. We were getting nearly **12–13 hours of daylight**, which made exploring much easier.

In the evening, we visited **Shanti Stupa**, perched high above the city. It's about **800 meters above town**, and from there, you can see the **entire Leh city view**. The view was incredible. We could even trace the road leading up to **Khardung La**, which we were set to conquer the next day. As the sun began to set behind the mountains, the sky turned golden, and the wind carried the faint flutter of prayer flags. We sat quietly, soaking it all in.

That night, we slept early. For real this time.The next day, **the real Ladakh circuit ride would begin**.

"Lost in the vastness of
Leh, finding
Myself amidst the
Mountains"

CHAPTER FOUR

KHARDUNG LA AND NUBRA VALLEY

It was a crisp morning in Leh, the kind where the chill in the air nudges you awake even before the alarm rings. At **7:00 AM**, we checked out of our hotel, our breath forming faint clouds as we loaded the bikes. Our luggage was tightly secured with bungee cords, jackets zipped up, gloves on, helmets clicked into place—we were ready. This wasn't just another ride. Today, we would cross **Khardung La**, one of the highest motorable passes in the world, standing tall at **17,982 feet**.

We had a plan. Our bike formation was simple but effective: **Gaurav** led the way, **Suraj** stayed in the middle, and I took the rear—keeping an eye on both of them. It gave us a sense of balance and control, which is vital on such unpredictable terrain.

Our final destination for the day was **Hunder village**, nestled in the **Nubra Valley**, about **120 kilometres** away from Leh. On any regular highway, which would be a short three-hour ride. But this wasn't any regular highway. We had heard stories—of treacherous roads, steep inclines, thin air, and sudden weather shifts. We weren't in a rush, and we weren't looking for speed. This was about the experience, the journey, the mountains.

Since we were starting early, we decided to skip breakfast and grab something along the way. The first **15 to 20 kilometres** were deceivingly easy. The tarmac was smooth, the bikes purred, and the sun slowly crept above the horizon, casting golden light over the stark, rocky terrain. But as we started ascending, the road began to deteriorate. Asphalt gave way to loosen gravel, dust clouds, and scattered stones. The curves grew sharper. The air, thinner.

The **BRO (Border Roads Organisation)** had clearly done their best to maintain the path, but nature has its own plans up here. Snow, landslides, and harsh winds constantly wipe away whatever progress is made. We saw workers, shovels in hand, repairing sections with nothing but grit and determination. In some parts, there was no road at all—just dust trails and scattered boulders.

Our pace dropped significantly. We were barely hitting **25 km/h**, struggling to even shift to third gear on the steep climbs. The road snaked up relentlessly, and every bend revealed either a spectacular view or a brutal stretch of broken path. Still, we kept going.

By the time we reached **South Pullu**, it was around **9:30 AM**. This is a military checkpoint where you need to show your **Inner Line Permit**—a document that grants you access to border-sensitive regions like Nubra Valley—and the **bike rental receipts**. It also became our impromptu breakfast stop. We found a tiny roadside shack serving **bread omelette and steaming hot chai**, which at that moment felt like the finest meal we'd had in days.

As we sat on small wooden benches, sipping tea and gazing at the snow-peaked ridges, we felt the temperature continue to drop. From the relatively mild **12–13°C** back in Leh, it was now hovering around **7–8°C**. And we still had more to climb.

After a good hour of rest, we hit the road again. The ride toward Khardung La Top was as challenging as it was exhilarating. Our bikes bounced over rocks and mud. The wind was now colder, sharper. Yet, the views—oh, the views—were otherworldly. Towering mountains stretched into the horizon, clouds lazily clung to their peaks, and prayer flags flapped in the breeze, as if cheering us on.

Eventually, we made it. **Khardung La Pass**, at the top of the world. The signboard greeted us like an old friend—bright yellow, covered in stickers and scribbles from countless others who had made the journey. At 17982 **feet**, the air was razor-thin, and every step took effort. But we felt alive—more than ever before. We parked the bikes, took a few photos, shared some high-fives, and just stood there for a while, breathing it in. It wasn't just the altitude that left us breathless—it was the moment.

But we couldn't linger for long. The winds picked up, and the chill started to bite. We began our descent—a whole different challenge. The road was just as unforgiving on the way down. Sharp turns, gravel slides, and the occasional speeding **local taxi** made the ride feel like a video game with real stakes. These drivers, so used to these mountain roads, zipped past with ease. For us, it was nerve-wracking, and we stayed alert, hugging the corners, using engine braking as much as possible.

After about **15 kilometres'**, we reached a small spot near **North Pullu**. Here, we stopped for tea again. This time, it was **Kashmiri Kahwa**, a spiced green tea with almonds and saffron. While sipping the warm, aromatic drink, I noticed something I'd never seen before—**a herd of yaks**. Massive, shaggy beasts with curved horns and thick fur, grazing calmly in the distance. They looked majestic, perfectly at home in this harsh, high-altitude landscape. That was my first time seeing yaks, and it felt surreal.

We mounted our bikes again and rode on. The terrain began to change—less snow, more sand, and shrubs. We were descending into **Nubra Valley** now, and the air grew warmer, the skies clearer. But the roads remained treacherous. Some sections were pure off-road—stones, loose gravel, and sudden drops that tested both skill and nerve.

The most adrenaline-pumping stretch was one where the road curled in a continuous zigzag, climbing up and down like a snake in motion. Every turn was a test of reflexes. Every blind curve, a gamble. That kind of speed, on that kind of road—it was madness. And yet, oddly impressive.

Around **3:00 PM**, we rolled into the breathtaking expanse of **Nubra Valley**. The landscape was unlike anything we had seen so far—lush green patches surrounded by barren mountains, sand dunes in the distance, and a quiet, almost sacred stillness in the air. We took a quick lunch break at a roadside eatery. The food was simple but hearty—dal, rice, sabzi, and hot chapatis. Just what we needed.

Our final leg was a **40-kilometer** ride to **Hunder village**. This was the most enjoyable stretch. A straight road, almost **10 kilometres** long, cutting through the valley like a ribbon. On either side, mountains loomed like ancient guardians. I felt like I could spread my arms and take off. The road soon curved again, and Gaurav and I leaned into the turns, touching **40–50 km/h**, feeling the rhythm of the ride. That was the magic moment—the pure joy of the open road, surrounded by the Himalayas.

Himalayan 411, and at that point, I gained even more respect for the machine. It had carried me across some of the toughest roads on Earth, without complaint. Suraj was a bit slower, but that was his comfort zone, and we never forced pace. Adventure is personal, and everyone experiences it differently.

We reached our hotel in Hunder at **4:30 PM**. From the outside, the **luxury tents** looked impressive lined up neatly, with flags fluttering and a signboard welcoming guests. But inside, it was a different story. The tent had large gaps at the bottom, freezing air blew in from the back, and there was no table or place to keep our stuff. I was disappointed. After such an epic ride, we'd hoped for a bit of comfort.

But then again—that's what adventure is. It doesn't come wrapped in comfort or predictability. It comes in dust-covered roads, gasping breaths at high altitude, and imperfect tents at the end of a long day. And we wouldn't have it any other way.

That evening, we decided to take it slow. After the long ride into Hunder, we spent time just unwinding at the property there were apple trees, pears, peaches but not ready to harvest. As night fell, we headed to the **Bonfire Resort Café**, a charming little restaurant run by locals. The warmth of the **hot food**, the gentle **sound of the nearby stream**, and the **live music** created a calming vibe. We sat under an open sky filled with stars, the fire crackling gently beside us. It was peaceful, raw, and real—the kind of evening you don't forget.

Came back to the resort, someone from the staff informed us that the **electricity would be cut at 10:00 PM and wouldn't return until 5:00 AM**. It was a remote region, and that was normal. We quickly got everything set for the night—charged our devices, found our flashlights, zipped up our tents. But something was off. There were **lots of insects** around the tents—strange bugs that made us uncomfortable. We informed the management, but they seemed helpless. The lights went out, and with them, our sense of safety.

Still, exhaustion eventually took over, and we slept.

The next morning, the air was brisk and cool. We got ready early, planning to explore more of **Nubra Valley**. We skipped breakfast at the resort and instead stopped at a tiny spot in **Diskit village**, just **10 kilometres away**, for some warm chai and local snacks.

Soon after, we made our way to the **Diskit Monastery**—a place that instantly silenced the mind. Perched high on a hill, the monastery overlooked the vast Nubra Valley, with the **Shyok River** winding through it like a silver thread. A massive **statue of Buddha** sat peacefully, his gaze stretching toward the horizon. We spent time just sitting, **meditating**, and soaking in the stillness. There was something sacred about that place—something that words can't quite capture.

We returned to the resort around **12:00 PM** and decided to explore the living area of the property.

Inside, there was a **carrom board**, **table tennis**, a **guitar, books**, and even a **canvas for painting**. It was a cozy little hangout zone. We played carrom—Gaurav won. Then came table tennis—I was the winner. The afternoon was full of jokes, teasing, and laughter, especially between Suraj and Gaurav. At one point, **gaurav** sat quietly and started sketching. On the canvas, he painted a bike riding through the rugged roads of Ladakh—a perfect symbol of our journey.

Around **5:30 PM**, we left for the **sand dunes of Hunder**. Unlike typical desert, Hudner's sand dunes are part of a cold desert ecosystem offering a surreal experience of white sands amidst towering peaks. As we reached a ridge at an altitude of nearly **10,000 feet**, we stood still. If you closed your eyes and just listened, you could imagine being on a beach, far from the mountains.

We spotted **Bactrian camels**—majestic creatures with two humps, remnants of the ancient Silk Route caravans. Some tourists were riding them, but we preferred to just watch from a distance. I found a quiet spot in the dunes, sat down, played some **music**, and closed my eyes.

Nubra valley wasn't just a destination for me – it was a walk into the depths of my own heart. As I stood among the surreal landscape memories from my past came rushing back like a silent tide it reminded me of a dream. I had once held close. my favourite dream which remained incomplete yet never forgotten. In that moment it felt as if my heart blossomed like a Cherry Tree full bloom touched by the magic of the place. my soul wondered not just through the valley but towards someone presence memory perhaps even a feeling that still leaves deep within me someone who remains special eternally till my last breath. I felt that moment incredibly special and never ending…………..

It was **Suraj** who shook me out of the trance. I hadn't realized how long I'd been lost in thought. Without saying a word, I told them, "Let's Walk."

We walked for nearly **three kilometres'**, side by side, but in silence. None of us spoke. I was trying to piece together the moment that had just passed something stirred deep within me the memory did not come back as a clear picture but rather as a wave of feeling rock overwhelming and incredible it was as if something had quietly shifted inside me something I haven't even know was missing I felt whole grounded like wondering soul finally finding its place it was a rare kind of fulfilment Like discovery a single green shoot thriving in a barren desert and gently pouring water over it Quite rebirth a silent joy blooming in an Unexpected place. The mountains around us, the fading sunlight, the wind whistled across the desert carrying the sound of sand grains moving—it said everything.

At one point, we came across a **small mountain stream**. We removed our shoes and dipped our feet into the icy water. It was **freezing**, but in the best way—like nature's own therapy. We just sat there, legs in the stream, water flowing past, and for a while, time didn't matter.

By **7:00 PM**, the light began to fade, and we headed back. On the way, we stopped for dinner at a roadside dhaba. The food was simple but delicious. Back at the resort, we requested a **change of rooms**—the previous tent had been too exposed. The manager hesitated at first, but after some convincing and checking availability, he shifted us to a **"Dormitory Tent"**, which was far better. We finally felt settled.

Before going to bed, the manager gave us a heads-up:

"The road to **Pangong Lake** has **multiple water crossings**. You must leave early. Once the sun rises, **glaciers start melting**, and the water level increases, which can make the roads impassable."

We nodded, unaware of just how **thrilling and dangerous** the next day would be.

We set the alarm for **5:00 AM**. Tomorrow's ride would cover **200 kilometers**, and though Google Maps showed **six hours of travel**, we knew better. In Ladakh, time and distance are ruled by terrain—not clocks.

And so, we slept, not entirely at peace, but eager for whatever lay beyond the mountains.

"YOU ARE THE SMILE I NEVER OWN,

A LOVE I FEEL, YET STAY UNKNOWN"

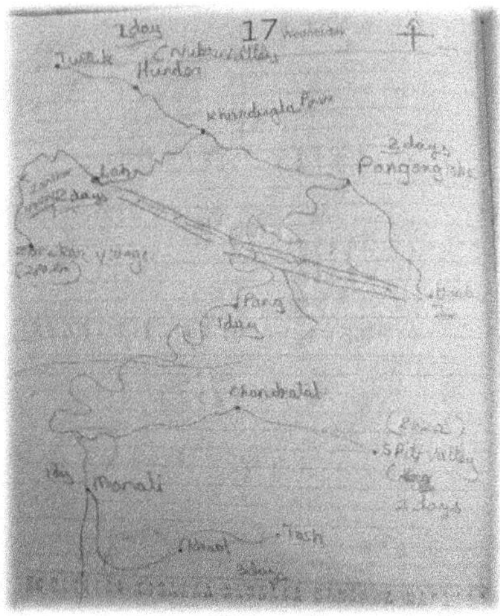

This is a rough road map of Ladakh and himachal
which was revised with Ladakh Only.

**1)Thukpa and Momos at Lamayuru Restaurant
2)English breakfast at Montagne Contemporary
Café**

Shanti Stupa

Gaurav, I, Suraj ready for the rid

I, Gaurav, Suraj at khardug la (Animation
image)

Nubra valley view from Diskit monastery

Buddha statue

Pangong Tos

Water crossing near Spangmik village

Washed out road near merak village

Pangong Tos view form Rangjon resort

Road to Hanle through sands

Indian astronomical observatory at the peak of hill in Hanle.

Rezang La war memorial, Ahir dham. 1962 Indo-china war.

Hanle village

Cattle Grazing in Hanle village

CHAPTER FIVE

PANGONG LAKE BLUE BEYOND BELIEF

22 July We woke up early at 5:00 AM, quickly got ready, and loaded our luggage onto the bikes. By 5:30 AM, we were ready to hit the road. Today wasn't just any ordinary day — it was Gaurav's birthday, and we were about to have the perfect outing by Pangong Lake. We wished him and set off towards our destination, with excitement and anticipation building up for the ride ahead.

We stopped at the same hotel for breakfast where we had lunch a few days ago — a place serving delicious bread omelettes and parathas. We quickly had a bite, and then I confirmed the road conditions to Pangong. The hotel owner mentioned that the original route was blocked due to landslides and stones, but luckily, an alternative road had just been opened about a kilometre back, thanks to coordination from the Indian Army. This new path would eventually reconnect to the original road after crossing the Shyok River, so we were thankful to the local for guiding us and saving us valuable time.

However, as we were about to leave, Gaurav couldn't find his bike keys. We searched everywhere, even wondering if the dogs might have taken them! We spent a good 10 to 15 minutes scouring every corner, while Google searches and frantic thoughts added to the pressure. Finally, just when we were about to give up, Gaurav said "sapadli" found the keys in the pocket of his riding jacket. Relieved, we got back on track.

This diversion had added around 20 extra kilometres to our journey, and the roads were still tough. At times, the river crossing was difficult and slow, and we faced challenges due to the constantly shifting terrain. Suraj's bag even fell off at one point, but I managed to grab it, and we secured it tightly. As we passed Tsati village, road was worst.

By the time we reached the Rongdu Bridge, which would connect us back to the original Pangong route, we had been riding slowly for hours. The moment we crossed the bridge, we decided to take a break, hydrate, and enjoy the view of the road ahead. The landscape was amazing, and the roads had improved, so we started cruising at around 45 km/h. The feeling of the open road, the mountains surrounding us — everything felt right.

But then, we saw it: the first major water crossing. It was a tricky spot. Four bikes and one car had gathered near the crossing. We all waited for the car to go first, trying to gauge the depth and assess the best way to cross. When a local Alto came, we watched carefully as the driver navigated the crossing. From that, I quickly calculated the depth and assessed the situation — the water was muddy, and in some places, it was 3 to 4 feet deep. We knew we had to proceed cautiously.

I decided to go first. With my bike in first gear, I slowly made my way through the water, keeping steady acceleration and avoiding looking down. It felt like a nightmare in slow motion, but within seconds, I had crossed. One by one, Gaurav and Suraj followed. As I helped them, a fourth biker asked if I could guide him through. His wife was too scared to attempt it, so they requested to follow the local car, and she got into the car to cross.

It felt like an intense and rewarding experience. After crossing, the local driver thanked us, and we all shared a quiet moment of camaraderie, grateful that we had helped each other through this challenge.

As we continued our journey, I felt the true essence of camaraderie — helping each other out not for the reward, but simply for the smiles. After the water crossings, we made our way towards our next destination. Along the way, we encountered several smaller water crossings, but nothing as challenging as the previous one. By around 11:00 AM, we reached Shyok village.

At this point, we were about to tackle some steep climbs and winding curves, and the view was simply breathtaking. The roads were more challenging, but the scenery kept us going. The water was crystal clear, and I was surrounded by the rugged beauty of Ladakh. In Ladakh, there's a beautiful tradition — when bikers pass each other on the road, they wave their hands as a sign of respect. I loved this simple yet meaningful gesture. It reminded me of the unity and respect among riders here, and it felt nice to be a part of it.

By 1:30 PM, we arrived at Tangtse village. We stopped to fuel our bikes first, then ourselves. Since we still had to cover about 65 kilometres', we decided to have some dal chawal (lentils and rice) and fresh akh (bread). We ate in the sun, drying out our wet shoes and socks, and enjoying a much-needed break. After our rest, we got back on the road. The last stretch was one of the most beautiful parts of the journey. The road was smooth, and the views were even better.

As we rode through the final stretch, a sudden curve in the road opened up a view I will never forget — Pangong Lake. For a moment, time stood still. The lake stretched endlessly before me; I was surprised by its deep blue colour. It looked like a lake of ink, glowing in shades of blue I didn't even know existed. It wasn't just water; it looked like liquid sapphire poured across the valley floor, reflecting the cold sky and surrounded by silent, towering mountains.

The first thought that crossed my mind was: *Is this even real?* It felt like a dream, a painting brought to life — so still, so perfect, so untouchable. The contrast of the arid mountains with the vibrant lake created a scene so surreal that I had to blink twice to believe it. The wind was sharp, but I didn't care. I took off my helmet, closed my eyes for a second, and breathed in the crisp, thin air. The silence was deep — the kind that echoes in your soul.so vibrant and mesmerizing that it was almost surreal.

I had seen photos of Pangong before, but nothing could have prepared me for this. That first sight wasn't just a view — it was a feeling. A kind of peace I hadn't known I was missing. In that one moment, all the exhaustion from the ride, the cold, the bumpy roads, the water crossings — it all vanished. It was just we three, the lake, and the infinite sky.

Our resort was located in Merak village, just 10 kilometres away from Spangmik village. This 10-kilometer stretch was one of the best parts of the entire ride. The road was beautiful, with small water crossings that didn't slow us down. But just 2 kilometres from Merak, we hit a patch where the road was completely washed away by the heavy flow of water. We had no choice but to take an alternative route, crossing over stones and water. It wasn't easy, but somehow, we made it through.

Once we reached the resort, we completed the check-in process and took the much-needed hot shower after such a tough ride. However, there was something we hadn't anticipated — in the Pangong region, there was no network or internet connectivity, which was quite a challenge. Gaurav and Suraj were especially upset by this, as they had been hoping to connect with their families. The local SIM card we had bought in Leh was useless, and Gaurav was feeling nervous because he hadn't been able to reach his parents, who might be wating for his call to wish him.

Suraj and Gaurav went to the only shop in Merak village to make calls, but the shopkeeper was in cooperative. They returned frustrated, and Gaurav, in particular, felt anxious and upset. After resting for a couple of hours, we decided to head out for a walk to clear our minds.

In the evening, the owner of the resort, a humble man from Leh who had leased the land, returned. We had a nice conversation with him, during which we learned that only a select few locals had been given SIM cards for the region. The owner kindly offered to help us, allowing us three phone calls to our families. Gaurav was overjoyed to hear from his parents. We all took turns calling home, letting our loved ones know that we would be out of contact for the next couple of days.

During our conversation with the owner, he shared some fascinating details about the region. He explained how close China's border was, and how certain areas were restricted by the army. We also learned that, due to the proximity to the border, the region was heavily monitored, and security was strict. He also told us the depth of the lake is uncounted, and the water is salty. The also shared the experience during the conflict with china. He even told us about winter the lake is frozen that one can walk on its Indian army conducts marathon over it. All this conversation went for a long time. I understood how beautiful and challenging this condition was.

Afterward, Suraj went to sleep, as he was feeling a bit tired, while I & Gaurav decided to head down to the lakeside. The sunset over Pangong Lake was a perfect end to the day. For a brief moment, I felt like I could stay there forever, just taking in the tranquil beauty. But as it grew darker, we made our way back to the resort.

Later, we had dinner at 8:00 PM, where we met some new guests — three friends from Bengaluru, aged between 40 to 45. They had hired a Thar from Kargil and had endured a rough journey. We had a friendly conversation, and I helped guide them with advice about the roads and conditions, as they were heading back the next day. whenever I hear about Bangalore I feel happy as it's my second home another beautiful city which has a special place in my heart so discussion with them lasted long they were planning to go by khardungla pass but that was too long and a hectic journey I suggested them the chang la pass route where the road conditions were good add time would be saved they asked us about our journey and a further plans all this continued throughout the dinner.

Back in our room, the best part of the resort was the incredible view. As we lay in bed, we could see Pangong Lake from one side and a star-filled sky from the other. The roof had a huge glass panel, and the windows were wide open, offering the most stunning view. This view was a paradise for me as I like star gazing and the view provided in your bed was icing on the cake I honestly don't remember when we finally fell asleep that night.

We woke up around 8:00 AM, refreshed and ready to start the day. By 10:00 AM, we were headed to breakfast. The meals were included in our stay, and we figured a heavy breakfast would be the best way to begin our day. We sat in the gazebo, enjoying the beautiful weather and the peaceful silence of the area. There were only three of us, the chef, three helpers, and the owner, on the property.

Suraj and Gaurav stayed at the gazebo for about an hour, chatting and soaking in the atmosphere, before heading back to the room due to the freezing wind. I decided to take a different approach — I opted to read a book in the living area. I was reading *The Year of Living Danishly*, a book about Denmark, and as the name suggests, it was all about Scandinavian culture. I found myself absorbed in it for a couple of hours.

Around 3:00 PM, I decided to take a power nap to recharge for the rest of the day. By 5:30 PM, we were ready to explore again. We made our way to a spot by the lake where we could walk along the shores and truly feel the moment. It was peaceful, and I spent some time clicking photos, capturing the beauty of Pangong Lake. I sat there for a while, letting the serene surroundings sink in, before heading back to the resort.

As we walked back, I found myself reflecting on the time spent with my friends. Suraj and I have known each other since school, and though Gaurav and I were also school friends, but Suraj and I shared a special bond. We knew everything about each other, and it was comforting to reminisce about old memories. We laughed and joked like we had never stopped, picking up right where we left off. It was one of those moments that made everything feel special. The time flew by, and soon it was getting dark, so we had to walk back to the resort.

Once back in the room, we relaxed for a bit before heading to dinner. Tonight, the property was bustling with families, and soon a buffet was set up. The wind was growing harsher as the night progressed, so we packed our bags for the journey ahead. Despite the cold, we couldn't help but enjoy the view and the quiet beauty of the place. We ended the evening feeling content, with the promise of more adventures tomorrow.

"Friendship isn't about who.

you spend the most time with.

It's about who you have the

best time with."

CHAPTER SIX

HANLE — DARK SKY

It was 8:00 AM when we left Pangong behind and set out on one of the most remote and demanding legs of our journey — toward Hanle, home to India's first Dark Sky Reserve. Before setting out, we had requested an early, heavy breakfast knowing well there would be no food, fuel, or civilization for the next several hours.

After our permits were checked at Chushul, we were warned: *'There's nothing ahead for 60 kilometres'* — no *shops, no people, no help. Just sand, dust, and the wind."* The officer's words were simple but loaded. What we didn't realize then was that those 60 kilometres would be among the most demanding and surreal parts of our entire Ladakh journey.

As we crossed the last few signs of habitation in Chushul, the road simply ceased to exist. There was no tarmac, no gravel — just an open expanse of loose sand stretching into the horizon, with only faint tyre impressions from earlier vehicles hinting at a possible direction. It felt less like a road and more like a forgotten trail across a desert battlefield.

Riding in sand isn't just tricky — it's mentally exhausting. The moment you lose focus; the bike starts sliding. Your front wheel sinks or skids, and panic kicks in. We had to keep our bodies loose, our hands steady, and our minds sharp. Every metre required calculated balance. Speed was not an option. We barely crossed 15 kmph. The bikes were constantly swaying, the front tires carving paths through the soft surface, threatening to buckle with every uneven patch.

There were moments when the rear wheel spun in place, and we had to stop, dig it out, push, and try again. The weight of the luggage didn't help, and neither did the high altitude. Every action — lifting the bike, dragging a foot to stabilize — left us winded and gasping. We didn't talk. We couldn't. It took everything just to stay upright and moving.

The wind howled across the plain. It wasn't violent, but constant — a dry, whispering presence that carried sand into our helmets, our eyes, and even our water bottles. The sky above was brutally clear, the sun stark and unforgiving. There was no shade, no trees, not even a shrub. Just an endless desert of silence — a silence so deep that even the thump of our engines felt out of place.

Now and then, we'd spot a BRO (Border Roads Organisation) sign hammered into a rock or a lone marker half-buried in sand, reminding us we were still on a military-maintained route. Once or twice, we passed by groups of BRO workers who waved at us — their faces covered in cloth, their eyes barely visible from behind goggles. They looked like ghosts of the land, quietly carving roads out of nothing, one shovel of sand at a time.

About halfway through, we came across an unexpected sight — a shallow lake shimmering under the harsh sun. It should've been beautiful, but the situation there was tense. A white Fortuner SUV was stuck badly in the wet, muddy banks of the lake. The vehicle had sunken halfway into the slush, and three men stood outside, covered in mud, arguing and trying everything they could to get it out. The more they tried to accelerate, the deeper the vehicle sank.

We stopped and offered help. Pushed. Pulled. Suggested. Nothing worked. It was clear that brute force wasn't going to solve this — they needed a tow, or at least another big vehicle. Making it worse, the army convoys we flagged down refused to stop. Perhaps out of protocol, perhaps suspicion, or maybe just the harsh reality of this region — help is a privilege, not a guarantee. The three men were panicking, shouting over each other, and with no teamwork, they were going nowhere.

We told them we'd send help if we could, and left, reluctantly. Barely three kilometres' ahead, I heard a familiar metallic clank — the sound of a JCB excavator working on a slope. I immediately rode up to the driver, explained the situation, and to my relief, he agreed to help. I pointed him in their direction, hoping he'd get there in time.

Back on the trail, the sand resumed its slow assault. There were long stretches where the ground was so fine and deep that the bikes felt like they were swimming in it. At one point, I thought my clutch had burned out. The engine was screaming, but the bike barely moved. I had to ease off, find a rhythm again, and just... keep going.

It was in this silence, this nothingness, that we utterly understood what isolation felt like. The sandy road demanded your full attention, and offered nothing in return — no signs, no voices, no comforts. Just a constant whisper from the wind, and the endless crunch of wheels against the earth.

As we made our way through the cold, barren landscape of chushul, the road led us to one of the most emotional stops of our journey – The Rezang la war memorial. Surrounded by silent mountains and an overwhelming stillness, the place holds a powerful energy that instantly commands respect. Standing there, remembering the brave 114 soldiers of 13 Kumaon regiment who laid down their lives in the 1962 war with china, we were struck by the sheer courage it must have taken to hold their ground against impossible odds. A salute to the spirit of those who gave everything for the country.

But Ladakh has a way of rewarding patience. Near the end of the stretch, as we neared Rezang La, we suddenly spotted movement on the horizon — dozens of *kiangs*, Indian wild asses, scattered across the landscape. Beautiful creatures, strong and elegant, they darted across the sand in graceful motion. For a moment, we forgot the heat, the tiredness, the aching arms. Nature had offered us a rare gift in the middle of nowhere.

Finally, we reached **Loma Bridge**. The narrow metal bridge spanned a dry gorge, and just across it stood another army checkpoint. We parked the bikes, pulled off our helmets, and took a deep breath. It felt like reaching an island after drifting through a desert sea.

Crossing the narrow **Loma Bridge** felt like stepping into another world. The check post on the other side was quiet but well-guarded. We were asked to dismount, show our permits, and enter all our details in a register — name, vehicle number, identification, and intended destination. It was a reminder that we were in one of the most sensitive and remote zones of India, where every movement is tracked, and every visitor accounted for.

Once cleared, we started riding again. To our relief, the road ahead was much better. Smooth stretches appeared like a reward after the relentless sandy torment of Chushul. But despite the better surface, we were all utterly exhausted — mentally, physically, emotionally. The sun was high, our limbs sore, and our backs stiff. All we needed was a moment to breathe.

And then, almost like a gift from the journey itself, we found it — just 10 kilometres from the check post.

A **perfect riverside patch** — the **Sindhu River** flowing gently beside a lush grassland, with wild horses grazing nearby and the cool mountain breeze washing over us. It was surreal. We parked the bikes, ran toward the riverbank like children, kicked off our shoes, and collapsed onto the soft grass. That **one-hour break** felt sacred. We lay there silently, not speaking much, letting the wind and water take away the fatigue. No one wanted to leave — it felt like the most peaceful place on Earth.

But the road still called. Hanle was now just 30 kilometres away.

We mounted our bikes again, a little lighter, and rode the final stretch. At around **4:30 PM**, we reached the remote but serene **village of Hanle**, nestled in the Changthang region of Ladakh. There are no hotels in Hanle — only a few **homestays** run by local families. Ours was **Padma Homestay**, a modest but welcoming place.

We parked our bikes and were greeted by the owner — a kind- woman who offered us a room and served us hot **lemon tea**, which felt like life returning to our veins. One by one, we freshened up, removed our dusty riding gear, and stretched out to rest.

Just then, as I opened the door to let in some air, I saw a **woman standing outside**, visibly distressed. Her eyes were filled with worry, and she spoke in broken Hindi, crying and trembling. I gently asked her to calm down. Her story came out in pieces — she and her husband had gone to **Umling La Pass**, one of the highest motorable roads in the world. On the way back, she had sat in a **camper vehicle** while her husband rode alone behind her on a motorbike. She was supposed to be dropped off at a point where he would join her — but the driver brought her all the way to Homestay. It had been **two hours**, and there was still no sign of her husband.

We looked around. There was no network. No way to call or trace anyone.

She was panicking. **Suraj**, completely drained from the ride, stayed back in the room. **Gaurav and I** decided to help.

The challenge: There were **multiple roads** leading toward Umling La, and the woman had no idea which one her husband had taken. We asked locals, and one **Ladakhi lady pointed us to a possible route**. Gaurav took the woman and rode in one direction, while I took another.

A few kilometres in, I saw a **group of bikers** approaching. I slowed down and asked if they'd seen a **red Pulsar with a lone rider**. One of them nodded, "Yes, he's coming. Just a bit behind us." I turned the bike around and raced in that direction. And there he was — a dust-covered man, riding with a worried look.

I waved him down and explained everything.

He was relieved. "Yes, that's my wife," he said, nodding quickly.

We both headed back toward the homestay. **Gaurav** and the woman returned just 10–15 minutes later from the other direction. The reunion was emotional. She ran to him and broke down — a mixture of joy, relief, and fatigue. We didn't stay for the whole scene. We quietly slipped back to our room. Our job was done.

Later, the couple came to thank us — humbled and grateful. That small moment stayed with me. It reminded me that adventure isn't just about landscapes and thrill — it's about humanity. Sometimes, helping someone reunite is the most powerful part of a journey.

After the long day, my body needed rest more than anything. I took a quick **power nap for half an hour**, letting the silence of Hanle lull me into a rare kind of stillness. When I woke up, the sun was dipping low, and the sky had started turning amber. I decided to step out for a **walk through the village**.

Hanle was calm, almost meditative. Surrounded by brown-and-gold mountains, dotted with whitewashed homes, and overseen by the distant domes of the **Indian Astronomical Observatory**, the place looked like it had stood untouched by time.

As I walked slowly down the gravel paths, I watched the simple life unfold — **children playing games**, laughing, and chasing each other, **men bringing back cattle**, and **women finishing chores** for the day. The clang of bells, the rustle of grass, and the occasional bark of a dog created a soundtrack of peace. It all stirred something within me — a memory. It reminded me of **my own childhood**, helping my grandfather bring livestock back from the fields. That life — so far, yet so familiar — flashed before my eyes. I smiled, took a few photos, and soaked in the nostalgia.

By the time I returned to the homestay, **Gaurav and Suraj were up**, stretching and chatting by the window. We all sat for a bit, talking in hushed voices, as if afraid to disturb the sacred silence outside.

Then came **dinner** — simple, homemade, and full of warmth. Dal, vegetables, rice, and hot rotis prepared by our host's mother. No fancy spices, no presentation — just food that felt like home. As we ate together, there was something very grounding about sharing a meal in that quiet mountain house, with only the wind howling faintly outside.

After dinner, I stepped out to **wash my hands**, and as I looked up… I **froze**.

The sky — the *sky* — had come alive.

I've always loved **stargazing**, but what I saw that night wasn't just stars. It was a **living galaxy**. The **Milky Way** stretched like a giant river of silver across the heavens. The **Saptarishi (Big Dipper)** constellation was crystal clear, as were countless stars I didn't even know existed. I stood there, **completely still**, for what felt like minutes. I couldn't move. Couldn't speak.

I had never seen so many stars in my life.

It felt like the stars had **descended** — like the ground had melted into the sky. There was no light pollution, no background noise, no distractions — just us and the universe. That moment shook something inside me. I felt **blessed**. Not for what I had or where I was — but simply for being alive in that exact moment. In that small corner of the world, I felt **how small we truly are**, and how vast everything else is.

I sat down on the lawn watching shooting stars dart across the heaven. In that silence- It felt like that stood still. It wasn't just stargazing. It was something more. It was as if the universe was putting on a private show, and I was the only one in the audience.

Even scientist choose this spot to study sky and for good reason. Days almost no light pollution here. The sky is pitch black, the kind of black you rarely see anywhere else, and the stars scene impossibly close. Some even cast faint shadows on the ground.

Hanley give me one of the purest, most humbling experience of my journey. It wasn't just another stop- it was a moment that reminded me why I travel. To feel wonder. To feel silence, to feel the universe stretch out above me and to feel my place within it.

We all stood outside, speechless. At some point, **it felt like the stars had touched the earth**, and the sky had folded into the valley. A rare kind of magic was happening. We stayed out there **till 2:00 AM**, unable to leave the view. Only the sharp **cold winds** forced us back inside.

That night, I didn't just sleep. I surrendered. To the silence, to the beauty, to the humility that Hanle had shown me. I closed my eyes, and in the stillness behind them, the stars kept shining.

The morning, we left Hanle for Leh, the air was crisp and the sky a soft shade of blue. There was no rush — just a quiet understanding among the three of us that this ride was going to be different. **The journey back wasn't just a return to the city — it was a return to us**.

As the bikes rolled forward, we were surrounded by the ever-changing landscapes of Ladakh. **Mountains of every shade** — from sunlit gold to deep crimson — lined the road. The **Indus River** kept appearing and disappearing beside us, flowing gracefully through the rugged terrain, reflecting the sky like a moving mirror.

This stretch, more than any other, became a meditation.

The road was smooth, winding gently, as if **inviting us to breathe**. I slowed down, letting the wind brush my face, and let my thoughts wander — into the **past**, the people I had met, the choices I had made; the **present**, the friends riding beside me, the land beneath me, the moment I was fully immersed in; and the **future**, still unknown, but for the first time, not scary.

I felt something I hadn't felt in a long time — **peace**. Real peace. **The kind that seeps into your bones**, not from achieving something, but from accepting everything.

When I was riding through the mountains in those days, I felt as if the mountains were speaking to me there was a silent language in the wind in the echoes of my engine in the rhythm of the wheels turning on rough roots. To truly here them one needs a special sense an inner stillness a deeper understanding even when they appear barren and lifeless the mountains hold unmatched strength and timeless wisdom they have stood tall for centuries guarding our border without expecting in their quiet resilience they offer safe passage asking for nothing in return their present is so silent promise protecting of endurance of ancient stories untold.

Somewhere near Chumathang We're lucky enough to spot a Himalayan Marmot it was busy digging a hole in earth completely absorbed in its task but the moment we stopped our bikes to get a closer look it quickly disappeared into its burrow Vanishing as if it had never been there it was a brief yet delightful moment catching a glimpse of this shy furry creature in its natural habitat a local taxi driver smile and told us that Himalayan marmots are quite common across Ladakh and the Tibetan plateau but still for us travellers it felt like a rare and special site

By late afternoon, **Leh city appeared in the distance**, almost like a dream from another lifetime. As we entered the familiar lanes, the chaos of vehicles, shops, and people suddenly felt comforting. We checked back into our hotel, **The Himalayan Retreat**, where this incredible journey had once begun. There was something poetic about returning to the same place — but as different people.

"Call me an old soul,

but I find peace in nature,

night, moon, stars,

sunsets, breezes, books,

smell of rain"

CHAPTER SEVEN

ZANSKAR VALLEY &LEH OUTSKIRTS

We stayed in Leh for **four more days** and decided to explore beyond the usual. One morning, we rode out to **Zanskar Valley**, a destination that felt like another planet. Our target was **Chilling village** — a small, quiet place nestled in the valley, surrounded by towering cliffs and whispering winds.

Zanskar valley, Nested deep in the remote reaches of the Himalayan in Ladakh, the land of rugged beauty, spiritual serenity, and raw adventure. Surrounded by towering peaks and carved by the wild zanskar river, the valley is known for its Dramatic landscapes ancient monasteries like phugta and karsha and its isolated charm. Accessible only for a few months in the summer by treacherous mountain roads, and in winter by the famous chadar trek over the frozen river, zanskar offers an untouched timeless glimpse into Ladakh monastic traditions and harsh yet captivating terrain. It remains one of the last truly remote destination in the region preserving its culture and natural splendour.

We reached the **Chilling Waterfall**, a place known for freezing completely in winter. But during our summer visit, it was alive and flowing, cascading down like **a ribbon of light and sound**. We sat under the shade of a lone tree, the waterfall on one side, the **Zanskar River winding through the valley below**, and silence stretching all around us. **How time passed there — we had no idea.** It felt like life had paused to let us breathe. Time we were speaking about ride, landscapes, water crossing and all of these things I remembered one sign quote of Indian army.

"When you go home, tell them of us and say,

for their Tomorrow, we gave our today."

When you utterly understand these words, you'll know the sacrifice a soldier makes for his country. The time once gone can't be returned to a jawan. I hold a deep respect and unwavering admiration for armed forces in my life. I was Once an aspirant to join their ranks, and though life took me on a different path, that respect has remained- and will stay with me always.

This all took me back to the memories of my preparation of these exams and SSB interviews best part of past where I leaned discipline, self-confidence, courage, teamwork which are really helpful of my day-to-day routine. All this conversation was going on and felt nice.

By evening, we returned to Leh, tired but deeply content. For dinner, we chose the famous **Tibetan Kitchen**, known for its **gourmet Himalayan cuisine**. To our surprise, there were **more foreign tourists than Indians**, and the wait was almost an hour. But it was worth every second. The food —was **rich, comforting, and full of stories** from the mountains.

Back at the hotel, we didn't go to our rooms right away. We sat in the **lawn under the open sky**, surrounded by the cold breeze and warm memories. We spoke of old days, of school, of random moments that still made us laugh. Above us, the **stars returned for their nightly show**, and it felt like even the sky was listening.

That night, there was nothing left to prove or chase. **Only gratitude** — for the roads, for the bikes, for the land, and for each other

The next day was **Vijay Diwas**. All around the city, there was a sense of **energy and pride**, a patriotic buzz in the air. Flags fluttered, people gathered, and the atmosphere felt alive with the memory of heroes. It was the perfect day to reflect on **courage, sacrifice, and purpose**.

We spent the afternoon in our room, **watching movies like "LOC: Kargil" and "Border,"** letting the emotions soak in. Each scene reminded us of the land we had just travelled — the high passes, the army bases, the memorials. It wasn't just about tourism anymore; **it was about respect**

Next day, after days of high passes, off-road challenges, frozen lakes, and silent stargazing, we woke up the next morning in Leh with no rush, no schedule — just a desire to explore something close, calm, and meaningful. **Stok Village**, just **20 kilometres from the city**, felt like the right choice.

The ride was short, but beautiful. As we left Leh's main roads behind, the surroundings grew quieter. The mountains looked softer the sun warmer. **Fields of barley** stretched across the land, small Ladakhi homes dotted the valley, and prayer flags fluttered in the morning breeze.

Our first stop was the **Stok Monastery**, a quiet, peaceful site that dates back to the **14ᵗʰ century**. It rests on a hill overlooking the entire valley. But what really caught our attention was the **massive 71-foot seated statue of Gautam Buddha**, serene and golden under the sky. It was built between **2012 and 2015** and consecrated by **Dalai Lama** himself.

Standing in front of it, we fell into silence again — not the silence of exhaustion, but of awe. The statue seemed to smile at the valley, unbothered by time or change, radiating calm. We spent some time meditating there, each of us caught in our own quiet thoughts, as the monastery bells echoed softly in the background.

Later, we visited the **Stok Palace**, built in **1820 by King Tse pal Namgyal,** the last ruling dynasty of Ladakh. The palace had the charm of fading royalty — its museum filled with old thangkas, royal robes, and ancient weaponry. Walking through its wooden corridors and gazing out its traditional windows, we could almost hear the whispers of a different Ladakh — a Ladakh ruled not by roads and tourists, but by silence, ritual, and tradition.

It wasn't a long outing, but it was enough. **Sometimes you don't need to go far to travel deep.**

That night, as if following tradition, we returned to our favourite spot — **The Tibetan Kitchen**. This time, we decided to try something new and ordered **Bagleb,** a Tibetan stuffed bread. It was soft, flavourful, and comforting — just the kind of warmth we needed on our last night in Leh.

After dinner, we walked back slowly to the hotel, not because we were tired, but because **we didn't want the day to end**. Back at the lawn, under that same infinity sky, we sat together — three friends, no words needed. Just late-night laughter, stories, and quiet glances at the stars we had started to know.

I felt deeply about the behaviour of Ladakhi people- So grounded, humble, and full of warmth. Despite the challenges of living in harsh, high-altitude terrain, their hearts seemed softer than the winds that swept through the valley. There was a simplicity in their way of life that made me pause and reflect. Their smile was genuine, their greeting heartfelt, and their hospitality unmatched. Whether it was a cup of tea in a tiny mud house or helping hand during our journey, they give without expecting anything in return. Routed in the teachings of Tibetan Buddhism, the carried a peaceful aura-calm, respectful, and full of compassion. The spirit of community watches evident everywhere; people worked together, celebrated together, add resolve conflict with patient and wisdom. They lived close to nature, with a deep reverence for the environment, using what they had with care and gratitude. Their resilience was inspiring, and their humble demeanour left a lasting imprint on my heart.

Next day after the breakfast we just went for a city ride where we crossed king Singay Namgyal chowk, Kalachakra stupa, ITBP camp and then back to hotel.

That afternoon I spent some time reading books from the hotel's living area. The manager with a curious expression, asked me about our ride. I shared the details of our adventure, and our conversation continued for a long time.

By evening, we headed to the **Leh city market**, a colourful, vibrant place full of local crafts, woollen scarves, handmade prayer flags, and warm smiles. We picked out **souvenirs for family and friends** — tiny pieces of Ladakh to carry back home.

For our last dinner, we chose a new spot — **Chef's Kitchen**, a rooftop restaurant known for its view. And what a view it was: **the city shimmering under night lights, Leh Palace standing proud in the distance, Shanti Stupa glowing softly, and the silhouettes of mountains guarding it all**.

We ate slowly, not wanting the meal — or the moment — to end.

Back at the hotel, we started packing. Each item we folded had dust from the journey. Every zipper sounded like a farewell. The bikes, our loyal companions, were parked for the last time. **Padma Bhai**, who had arranged them for us, was scheduled to collect them the next day. We **left the keys at the reception**, like a silent thank you.

And just like that, **our journey through Ladakh was done** — a journey not just across landscapes, but **through friendship, silence, struggle, joy, and discovery**.

What we brought back with us couldn't be packed in bags — it was something far deeper. **A part of Ladakh now lived within**

"Traveling – it leaves you

speechless, then turns you

into a storyteller"

CHAPTER EIGHT

THE UNEXPECTED JOURNEY

29 July Our return flight was scheduled at 10:00 AM, and like any traveller at the end of a long journey, we were ready. Bags packed, hearts full, and minds slowly drifting back to the world waiting for us. We had breakfast, double-checked everything, and left the hotel around 9:30 AM for Leh airport. Everything felt calm, like a quiet goodbye from the mountains.

Until it wasn't.

The moment we reached the airport, we were stunned. **Chaos.** People everywhere. Lines overflowing. Screens flashing one dreaded word: **Cancelled.** One by one, all flights were grounded. Confused and panicked, we rushed to the indigo counter, but the scene was already wild — frustrated passengers, helpless staff, and growing uncertainty.

We called customer care. Two options: **reschedule the flight after four days** or **fly out of Srinagar —** which was **430 kilometres** away. Four days felt like forever. Srinagar became the only realistic option.

The reason for this mess? **Runway melting**. Yes, the intense Ladakhi sun had caused **overheating of**

the tarmac — the tar had literally softened, making it impossible for planes to land or take off. An act of nature, completely out of our control.

We didn't have time to waste. We began looking for a taxi to take us **directly to Delhi** — but quickly learned that **no one** drives that route directly. Our best shot was Srinagar or Manali. Manali was even farther — 510 kilometres' — and recent **cloudbursts and landslides** made that road even more uncertain.

So, Srinagar it was.

But now came the real challenge — **finding a taxi**. Prices were suddenly sky-high. Drivers were quoting ₹23,000 to ₹28,000, capitalizing on the desperate situation. Gaurav and Suraj were deep in negotiations. Meanwhile, I called our hotel manager at **The Himalayan Retreat**, and thankfully, he arranged a Mahindra Xylo for ₹18,000. We didn't hesitate — we took the deal.

By **1:00 PM**, we began our **unexpected road trip to Srinagar**.

At first, we were hopeful — Google Maps said it was a **10-hour journey**. That meant, if luck was on our side, we'd reach by 2:00 AM and could catch a morning flight. But the driver calmly shattered our calculations. Two major hurdles awaited us:

1. **Zoji La Pass** — one of the most dangerous passes in India, and closed to common vehicles at night.
2. **Amarnath Yatra Route Restrictions** — traffic towards Srinagar would only be allowed after **6:00 AM** due to Yatra security protocols.

This meant we would likely have to **halt at Dras**, the second-coldest inhabited place on Earth.

Just as we were digesting this news, the weather shifted. **Intense winds, dark skies** — a storm was brewing. Around **3:00 PM**, we stopped at **Khaltsi** for lunch. The atmosphere was so eerie, even the view from the window felt haunting. We barely ate — shared a simple **dal-chawal plate** among the three of us. But the driver insisted we eat something — the next proper stop was far away.

Bellies half-full, minds still racing, we took cash from an ATM, grabbed some water bottles, and hit the road again.

Soon after, we were stopped at a **check post**. A landslide had blocked the main road. The only way forward was through a **narrow, winding detour through remote villages**, which would add another **40 kilometres** to our trip. It was draining — physically, mentally — but our driver, a local from the Kargil region and an enthusiastic cricket player, kept our spirits lifted. His familiarity with the terrain was reassuring.

Through the dusty, snaking backroads, we talked. About his life, cricket, roads, and landslides. And then, like a movie twist, we hit **traffic again**. Another landslide. But this time, the **Border Roads Organisation (BRO)** was already at work. After about 30 minutes, the road was cleared, and we were back on the main route. **Kargil was still 60 km.**

We reached **Kargil** at 8:00 PM. The entire town was beautifully decorated for **Vijay Diwas the anniversary of India's Kargil war victory. Flags, light, and**

patriotic energy filled the streets. The driver had a brief stop to meet someone. We took a short break, soaking in the moment. It was surreal—so much pride, yet our minds were elsewhere, calculating our next move.

At around 9:30 PM, we stopped at a roadside Dhaba run by one of the driver's relatives. That's when we were told:
Zoji la Pass is closed at night.

Midnight at Zojila Check post
Despite the warnings, we pushed ahead. At **midnight**, we reached the **Zojila check post**. As expected, all vehicles were stopped. We begged the officer to allow us through. At first, he refused. But as we kept explaining that our flight was at 6:00 AM from Srinagar, he gave us a glimmer of hope: "Wait for an hour. I'll see what I can do."

While we waited, a **traveller van was allowed to pass**. Curious, we asked the officer why. His response was chilling—**the van was carrying a dead body**. Silence took over our car. A few minutes later, another vehicle passed with a similar reason. The weight of the situation, the late hour, the eerie surroundings, and the bitter cold—it all began to feel like a scene from a thriller movie.

We sat quietly in the car. No one spoke. The driver dozed off for a quick nap. At 1:30 AM, I returned to the officer with all our documents—flight booking, cancellation proof, and identity cards. This time, seeing our persistence, he nodded.
We were cleared to cross Zojila Pass at 1:40 AM.

The road through Zojila is one of the most dangerous

in India. Even in daylight, it's a terrifying drive—one side a steep drop, the other side rocky cliffs. At night, in fog and freezing cold, it felt ten times worse. We drove slowly, alert, praying silently.

Suddenly, in the foggy distance, a pair of glowing eyes appeared. It was **a Himalayan grizzly bear**—huge, majestic, and calm, almost as if it had come to silently bid us farewell. We saw it for just 10 seconds, but it felt like a moment suspended in time.

Amarnath Camp and Final Leg

As we descended, we saw the glowing lights of the **Amarnath Yatra base camp**, looking like a small city from above. We stopped at another check post around **4:45 AM**, but this time an officer stopped us.
"No vehicles move before 6:00 AM. Wait."

So, we waited—again.

At **6:00 AM sharp**, the gates opened. The driver, now fully awake and focused, drove like a champion. We had 90 km to cover and barely three hours left for our next flight.

Arrival in Srinagar

By 7:45 AM, we were in **Srinagar city**. First stop: ATM. We needed to pay the driver. Then we rushed to **Srinagar Airport**—arguably one of the most secure airports in India. Here, security begins before the gate: the car is inspected, luggage is scanned, passengers are verified—all before entering the main terminal.

We reached the **indigo counter** at 8:20 AM. Miraculously, tickets were available. ₹16,000 for 3 people—but we didn't think twice. We booked immediately, completed security checks, and waited for our boarding.

At **9:50 AM**, the flight took off.
As the plane soared into the sky, all three of us sat in silence. **32 hours. No sleep. No planning. Just instincts, brotherhood, and determination.** This was not just the end of our Ladakh trip—it was the conclusion of an adventure that had evaluated our courage, patience, and unity.

Sometimes, journeys choose you.
And this one—unexpected, thrilling, exhausting—will live in our heart's fore.

We landed in Delhi at **12 PM**. The moment we stepped out of the airport, it felt like we had entered a different world. **Hot, humid air** wrapped around us, a stark contrast to the cool, dry winds of Ladakh and the freezing pass of Zojila just hours ago. The city buzzed with traffic, crowds, and energy. But we were too drained to notice much—we just wanted to rest.

We had booked a hotel in **Connaught Place**, right in the heart of Delhi. As soon as we reached, we freshened up and headed out for **lunch at a Mughlai restaurant** nearby. The spices, the aroma, and the rich Flavors of the food felt heavier than usual—maybe it was exhaustion, or maybe our stomachs were still in mountain mode.

By **2 PM**, I crashed on the bed. **The exhaustion, the tiredness, the comfort of a mattress**—it was the perfect storm. I slept like I hadn't slept in days (because I hadn't). It was **Gaurav** who shook me awake at **10 PM**. I groaned, not wanting to move, but eventually got up. We stepped out again, had some **fresh lime water**, and tried something new—**tiger prawns**, battered fry. It was a small meal, but enough. We returned to the room, and this time, slept peacefully—no stress, no fear of missing flights, no freezing winds.

The next morning, I woke up at **8 AM**, finally feeling **recharged**. It was like all the exhaustion had evaporated overnight. Our first mission: **Sita Ram Diwan Chand**—the legendary chole bhature joint. And oh, it lived up to the hype. **Crispy, fluffy bhature** and spicy, tangy chole—the perfect breakfast to mark the last day of our journey.

We returned to the hotel, packed up, and got ready. Our flight to **Pune was at 3 PM**, so we left for the airport around noon. The Delhi airport felt different this time—less chaotic, more familiar. As we boarded, a sense of **peace** washed over me.

As the plane approached **Pune**, I looked out of the window. **Everything was lush green**—the **monsoon** was in full bloom. Hills, trees, rooftops… everything was soaked in nature's freshness. That moment, I felt something hard to describe—**a sense of return, of grounding, of home**.

We landed at **5:30 PM**.

The trip was over.

We stepped out, stood together one last time. We had shared **15 unforgettable days**, conquered landscapes, crossed rivers and passes, braved weather and fear. And now, it was time to part. We hugged, smiled, and said our goodbyes.

Everyone booked their cabs.

Everyone went their separate ways.

From being inseparable riders for two weeks, we were back to walking alone. But this time, with memories stitched into our souls and desire to re-visit this magical land again.

As I sat in my cab, watching the Pune rains, I whispered to myself—
"Till the next trip... goodbye."